Harlem
RENAISSANCE

Dona Herweck Rice

Consultant

Jennifer M. Lopez, NBCT, M.S.Ed.
Teacher Specialist—History/Social Studies
Office of Curriculum & Instruction
Norfolk Public Schools

Publishing Credits

Rachelle Cracchiolo, M.S.Ed., *Publisher*

Conni Medina, M.A.Ed., *Editor in Chief*

Emily R. Smith, M.A.Ed., *Content Director*

Véronique Bos, *Creative Director*

Robin Erickson, *Art Director*

Michelle Jovin, M.A., *Associate Editor*

Mindy Duits, *Senior Graphic Designer*

Image Credits: front cover (bottom left) Library of Congress, William P. Gottlieb Collection [LC-GLB13- 0421]; front cover (bottom right) LOC [LC-USZ62-127236]; pp.2–3 LOC, William P. Gottlieb Collection [LC-GLB23-1019 DLC]; p.5 (left) Newscom; p.5 (right) Lebrecht Music & Arts/Alamy; p.6 (left) LOC, General Collections [Digital ID # na0026]; p.7 (right) LOC [LC-DIG-ppmsca-38818]; p.7 (left) The University of Chicago Library; p.8 (right) LOC [LC-DIG-fsa-8c02701]; p.9 LOC [LC-USF33-020566-M4]; p.10 (left) LOC [E185 .5.06]; p.11 Archive Photos/Getty Images; pp.12–13 Valerie Gerrard Browne/Chicago History Museum/Bridgeman Images; p.13 (right) LOC [m1508.52922]; p.14 Eliot Elisofon/The LIFE Picture Collection/Getty Images; p.15 Stefano Bianchetti/Corbis via Getty Images; p.16 George Karger/Pix Inc./The LIFE Images Collection/Getty Images; p.17 (left) Gjon Mili/The LIFE Picture Collection/Getty Images; p.17 (right) LOC [LC-USZ62-39300]; p.18 LOC [LC-GLB13-0421]; p.19 Bettmann/Getty Images; p.19 (insert) Cab Calloway, "The New Cab Calloway's Cat-ologue/a Hepster's Dictionary" (Revised Edition, NY, 1939); p.20, p.25 (top right) New York Public Library; p.21 (left) National Portrait Gallery, Smithsonian Institution; gift of W. Tjark Reiss, in memory of his father, Winold Reiss. © Estate of Winold Reiss; p.21 (right), p.23, p.24 Carl Van Vechten photograph/Beinecke Library © Van Vechten Trust; p.22 New York Public Library/Science Source; p.25 (left) LOC [LC-USZ62-126945]; p.25 (bottom right) LOC [LC-USZ62-42529]; p.26 National Museum of American History; p.27 Weegee (Arthur Fellig)/International Center of Photography/Getty Images; p.29 LOC [LC-GLB23-0285 DLC]; p.32 (left) Indiana Historical Society; p.32 (right) LOC [m1508.52922]; all other images from iStock and/or Shutterstock.

Library of Congress Cataloging-in-Publication Data

Names: Rice, Dona, author.
Title: Harlem Renaissance / Dona Herweck Rice.
Description: 1st. | Huntington Beach : Teacher Created Materials, 2019. | Audience: Ages 7 | Audience: Grades 2-3 | Summary: "After years of oppression and slavery, a new day dawned for African Americans in the early twentieth century. An explosion of art, literature, music, and more swept the nation. In Harlem, New York, it was especially evident. It was there that a renaissance of art and thought caught the attention of the country and the world. Life was forever changed for both black and white Americans"-- Provided by publisher.
Identifiers: LCCN 2019024297 (print) | LCCN 2019024298 (ebook) | ISBN 9781425850678 (paperback) | ISBN 9781425850678 (ebook)
Subjects: LCSH: African Americans--Music--History and criticism--Juvenile literature. | Jazz--New York (State)--New York--1921-1930--History and criticism--Juvenile literature. | Jazz--New York (State)--New York--1931-1940--History and criticism--Juvenile literature. | Harlem Renaissance--Juvenile literature. | Harlem (New York, N.Y.)--Intellectual life--20th century--Juvenile literature.
Classification: LCC ML3508.8.N5 R53 2019 (print) | LCC ML3508.8.N5 (ebook) | DDC 780.89/9607307471--dc23
LC record available at https://lccn.loc.gov/2019024297
LC ebook record available at https://lccn.loc.gov/2019024298

TCM
Teacher Created Materials

5301 Oceanus Drive
Huntington Beach, CA 92649-1030
www.tcmpub.com
ISBN 978-1-4258-5067-8
© 2020 Teacher Created Materials, Inc.

Table of Contents

The A Train

The piano dives into a melody with a playful sweep of jitter and bounce. The piano notes are answered by a trumpeting blast of horns. Low and deep, the bass plucks a **syncopated** beat as the cool drum lays down a jolting rhythm. And while the music plays, Ella Fitzgerald stands poised at the microphone. She looks magnificent in a shimmering gown and a high hairdo. She begins to add a new instrument—her voice—to the melody. Fitzgerald weaves a spellbinding **scat**. But the horns are demanding, pushing Fitzgerald to slide and dive into the swinging lyrics of the classic jazz standard.

You must take the A train,

To go to Sugar Hill way up in Harlem.

If you miss the A train

You find you've missed the quickest way to Harlem.

Hurry! Get on now, it's coming.

Listen to those rails a-thrumming.

Oh boy, get on the A train.

Soon you will be on Sugar Hill in Harlem.

"Take the A Train" is an old-school jazz song. Billy Strayhorn wrote it for Duke Ellington and his **orchestra**. It became a signature song for both Ellington and Fitzgerald. Strayhorn wrote the song in a tribute to the New York City subway train he rode into Harlem, New York. He claimed that writing it felt just like writing a letter to an old friend.

Queen Ella

Ella Fitzgerald was a famous singer and was often called the Queen of Jazz. She performed all over the country, but she was especially known for performing at the Savoy Ballroom in the heart of New York City's Harlem neighborhood.

Sugar Hill

At the time that "Take the A Train" was written, Sugar Hill in Harlem was an upscale area. Billy Strayhorn and Duke Ellington, the famous jazz pianist and orchestra leader, lived there. In the 1930s and '40s, many wealthy African Americans made it their home.

▲ Fitzgerald sings in Harlem

5

A Renaissance in Harlem

Other Work

Du Bois helped found the National Association for the Advancement of Colored People (NAACP). He was also editor of its magazine, *The Crisis*. Du Bois published many Harlem Renaissance writers in the magazine.

Finding Harlem

Harlem is in Upper Manhattan (New York City). It is in between the Hudson River, the Harlem River, and the East River. Dutch sailors founded Harlem in 1658.

It wasn't just jazz singers who felt "called" to Harlem. From about 1918 to 1937, Harlem was home to a **cultural awakening**. This time was known as the Harlem Renaissance. Writers, artists, and scholars shined a light on black culture and emphasized racial pride. They also highlighted the problems that black people faced in the United States.

African American leaders, such as W. E. B. Du Bois (doo-BOYZ), began to gain fame. Du Bois spoke of how black people had suffered through the years of slavery. He spent his life trying to right those wrongs. Du Bois worked to form a world in which black people could live their lives fully. His book, *The Souls of Black Folk*, is still considered a masterpiece work on race. Du Bois's book focused on seeing African Americans as people. At the time he wrote the book, many people did not accept this fact. Deep racism was still rooted in American society.

▼ Du Bois in 1919

THE SOULS OF
BLACK FOLK

W.E.B.DuBOIS

Equality in the Arts

Great Migration

Many enslaved people saw the North as a way to find freedom. Then, in the post–Civil War era, the North continued to call to many people. People who had little money and those under threats of violence were especially drawn to it.

Jim Crow

The phrase "Jim Crow" probably comes from a racist character played by a white entertainer named Thomas Rice (shown above). In the 1830s, Rice created the Jim Crow character to make fun of black people and the president. He sang and danced while wearing **blackface**. He called the act "Jump Jim Crow." The phrase became popular throughout the segregated South.

Du Bois claimed that equality for all people would start in the arts. He wrote, "It is today that our best work can be done and not some future day or future year." Du Bois and other leaders believed that black people in Harlem would lead the way to a less racist, more equal country.

In response to these beliefs, bright and gifted black people moved to Harlem. Many of them came from the South in what is known as the Great Migration. They were trying to escape the unfair, racist Jim Crow laws that had taken over the South. Jim Crow laws were designed to keep black people from having the same rights as white people. After the Civil War and Reconstruction eras, Jim Crow laws

 A family moves north during the Great Migration.

made **segregation** legal. The laws took power from black people and gave it to white people. In this way, the old **social order** could continue, even without slavery. Recent social and political advancements were undone. The legacy of slavery lived on.

In Harlem, things were different. For many black people, Harlem was a safe place compared to the racism they likely would have faced in other cities.

▼ These men study the route from Florida to Delaware.

An Explosion of Culture

The explosion of black culture in Harlem was fast and widespread. The area was rich with new and creative forms of expression. Meanwhile, a growing community of African American people thrived and prospered.

Some white people also moved to Harlem. They were especially drawn to the music clubs, where jazz and blues were played to large crowds. At this time, mixed crowds of white and black people were nearly unheard of. In Harlem, music brought the two races together.

Of course, creating art was not new for the black community. But the amount of art *was* new. The volume of essays, books, music, and more was unlike anything that had come before in the United States. These art forms spread out from Harlem. Soon, people across the country and around the world were enjoying art from the Harlem Renaissance.

The artists and scholars of the Harlem Renaissance lit a flame. The flame, in turn, set off an explosion of culture.

Opportunity

Opportunity: Journal of Negro Life was published from 1923 to 1949. This magazine supported writers and artists of the time. It also helped to promote the new field of African American studies.

OPPORTUNITY
JOURNAL OF NEGRO LIFE

FEBRUARY 1926
INDUSTRIAL ISSUE

From Poverty to Prosperity

After its renaissance, Harlem fell into decline and poverty and became known for its high crime rates. But as with much of New York City, renewal followed. Today, areas in Harlem are some of the most desired properties in the city.

▼ Two guests at the Savoy Ballroom in Harlem dance to jazz music.

Beyond Harlem

While Harlem blazed with creative energy, it did not shine on its own. Throughout the country, the black community had found an outlet. The **oppression** of past decades was losing its hold. New art forms that began in black culture were spreading across the country.

The music of the renaissance—jazz and blues—was born outside of Harlem. The birthplaces of these musical **genres** could be found in Memphis, New Orleans, and other cities. Soon, jazz and blues spread like wildfire throughout the country. Musicians such as Jelly Roll Morton, Ma Rainey, and W. C. Handy brought the music to life. When jazz and blues finally made their way to Harlem, large crowds came to listen.

A few miles south of Harlem, a show on Broadway was taking the theater community by storm. It was the 1921 production *Shuffle Along*. This musical play brought jazz to theater. The show was also produced, written, and performed by African Americans. Crowds went wild for the groundbreaking new play.

This painting by artist Archibald Motley shows dancers at a jazz club in Chicago during the Harlem Renaissance.

Musical Revival

In 2016, *Shuffle Along* opened on Broadway once again. However, the new storyline is different. The original was about a campaign for mayor in a small town. The new show tells the story of how the 1921 production of *Shuffle Along* improved race relations.

Prosperity to Depression

After World War I ended in 1918, the United States became a leading world power. This helped many people become rich in the early 1920s. Later in the decade, financial growth slowed. When the Great Depression struck in 1929, it marked the beginning of the end of the Harlem Renaissance.

All That Jazz and the Crazy Blues

Louis's Early Life

Louis Armstrong has been called "one of the most influential artists in jazz history." For all his fame, however, Armstrong had a rocky start in life. He was born into extreme poverty and was forced to work as a child. When he was about 12 years old, he was sent to live in a home for young troublemakers. It was there that Armstrong learned how to play an instrument called a cornet. After that, Armstrong's love of music took off.

Sound the Horn!

One of the iconic sounds of jazz and blues music is the wail of a trumpet. Great musicians, such as Louis Armstrong and Dizzy Gillespie, made the trumpet sing through the Harlem Renaissance and beyond. However, the trumpet has a much longer history than the Harlem Renaissance. Records show that the first trumpet was invented around 1500 BC.

What exactly is jazz? Famous jazz singer Louis Armstrong is believed to have said, "If you have to ask what jazz is, you'll never know."

Jazz is a musical style that is largely American in origin. It comes mainly from African American musical traditions. Most likely it began in the South, near the beginning of the twentieth century.

▼ **Louis Armstrong**

There are a lot of types of jazz, which can make it hard to define. People sometimes say jazz is **improvisational**. Some people use terms such as **polyphonic** and **swing** when talking about jazz. Each of these terms is meant to capture the movement and feeling of jazz. For many people, jazz is one of those "I know it when I hear it" things.

However it is described, jazz was the soundtrack of the Harlem Renaissance. For some people, jazz *is* the Harlem Renaissance.

A close relation to jazz is the blues. The blues was born out of black culture in the South. The style can be traced back to the late nineteenth century. The blues is known for its sad-sounding bass. The blues also has emotional lyrics and repeating sounds. The blues began in African American spiritual music. It later branched out to form rock and roll and other genres.

The Savoy Swing

Part of what drew people to Harlem was the dance and music clubs there. The most famous clubs tended to be in the Lenox Avenue area. The "Jazz Age," as it was known, came into full bloom in places like the Cotton Club and the Savoy Ballroom, both located on Lenox Ave.

The Savoy was called the "soul of Harlem." It was a public ballroom where jazz musicians played. Massive crowds of people danced away each night to the swinging tunes. Four thousand dancers could fit into the block-long Savoy! It was packed every night. Black and white people alike danced there; the Savoy did not discriminate—unless a person could not dance well!

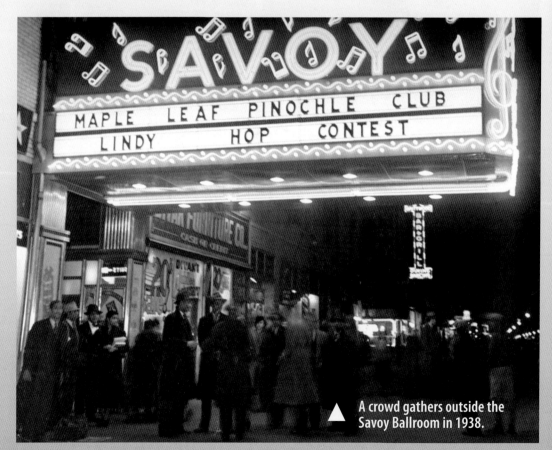

A crowd gathers outside the Savoy Ballroom in 1938.

Professional dancers demonstrate the lindy hop in 1943.

The Cotton Club

While the Savoy was open to all, only white people were allowed as guests in the Cotton Club. Many celebrities visited the Cotton Club to hear the latest jazz. One frequent visitor was baseball legend Babe Ruth. Ruth was at the top of his career during the Harlem Renaissance. He became close friends with both black and white performers at the Cotton Club and invited some of them to visit him in the Yankee clubhouse.

Lindbergh

In 1919, a hotel owner named Raymond Orteig announced a $25,000 reward (around $360,000 today) for the first pilot who could fly nonstop between New York City and Paris. Several pilots tried over the next few years but all failed. On May 20, 1927, Charles Lindbergh took off. More than 33 hours later, Lindbergh landed in Paris to a huge crowd of people. Lindbergh won the prize and was instantly famous for his daring trip.

The Savoy was known for its dancers, and **bouncers** would turn away people who couldn't keep up. A group of amazing dancers called the Savoy Lindy Hoppers could be found in the ballroom every night. The *lindy hop* is a style of dance with fast jumps and kicks, all while partners stay in contact. The style was born in Harlem. It gets its name from the famous pilot Charles Lindbergh, who was known as "Lucky Lindy." Lindy "hopped" the Atlantic Ocean in his plane—hence, the *lindy hop* name. People loved it, and lindy hop competitions became a regular event at the Savoy.

Jive Talk

In 1938, musician Cab Calloway created the first dictionary written and edited by an African American person. He called it *Hepster's Dictionary*. It is a glossary of jive—the language of jazz.

Jive is the lyrical slang heard in the world of the Harlem Renaissance. Like with other art forms of the period, jive language made its way into **mainstream** language and remains in use. Some people claim to be "beat" when they are tired. That term comes from jive. People who say they "had a ball" to describe having fun are using jive too. Something that's perfect is "in the groove," while looking neat and put together is to look "sharp." A person who can't hear something may ask you to "come again." At that, you can reply, "Yeah, man."

A Harlem "hep cat" (knowledgeable person) speaks perfect jive to every "jack and chick" (man and woman). He "breaks it up" (wins applause) by "jamming" (playing music) in a "killer-diller" (exciting) show. If you want to sound like a hep cat, "lay your racket" (talk jive) and show them that you "collar" (understand) it. You can "beat up your chops" (talk) until the "joint is jumping" (everyone is having a lot of fun).

Go ahead—"slide your jib" (talk freely)!

Lady Day

Billie Holiday is considered by many people to be one of the greatest jazz vocalists of all time. Nicknamed Lady Day, she was one of the first African American singers to work with a white orchestra. She had a very unique voice. Many people enjoyed her emotional interpretation of lyrics.

Cab Calloway

Calloway's breakout hit in 1931, "Minnie the Moocher," made him a huge star. Calloway played regularly at the Cotton Club and worked as both a singer and an orchestra leader. He was known especially for scatting, which he does in "Minnie."

Calloway and his band

A Dream Deferred

If music was the heart of the renaissance, then literature was its mind. Magazines like *The Crisis* were full of the **literary** works of black authors. Mainstream publishers began to print black authors' work in numbers never before seen. These printings played a role in making black authors famous around the world.

Harlem was also home to the birth of a literary genre. Just as jazz music came forward as a new type of music, jazz poetry was born as a new genre of literature. The rhythms of the poetry reflect the rhythms of the music. Jazz poetry—like jazz music—is also deeply based in black culture.

▲ Hughes (left) meets with other writers and community leaders in Harlem in 1924.

▲ This 1925 painting of Hughes hangs in the National Portrait Gallery.

Jazz poets became famous. One of those poets was Langston Hughes. Hughes's jazz poetry, novels, plays, and other works gained him fame. Hughes became known for his descriptions of black life in the United States. In his poem "Harlem," Hughes writes of "a dream **deferred**." The dream may be the equality black Americans had been denied. Hughes also asks whether a dream deferred might "explode." Maybe the Harlem Renaissance was the explosion Hughes was talking about.

The Dean

Alain Locke is sometimes called the **Dean** of the Harlem Renaissance. Locke was the first African American to be named a Rhodes Scholar. Rhodes Scholars are given a special two-year scholarship to Oxford University in England. Locke received this rare honor in 1907.

Thurman's Belief

Like Du Bois, many black writers thought their writings would convince people to change the old social order. A young writer and editor named Wallace Thurman challenged that idea. He believed that black writers should write whatever they wanted and not worry so much about what white people thought. Thurman's home in New York City became a meeting place for black writers to share their ideas.

Langston Hughes

Langston Hughes was born in Missouri but traveled to New York City to follow his dreams of being a famous writer. Hughes was a poet and a **playwright**. He also wrote essays and novels. A lot of his writing focused on the experiences of black people at the time.

Simple

In his column for the *Chicago Defender,* Hughes developed a character named Jesse B. Semple—better known as Simple. Simple was a type of black "everyman." Hughes used Simple to relate the everyday experiences of black Americans. He used Simple in later books and plays as well.

Unspoken Notes

When Hughes died in 1967, many people attended his funeral. Few words were spoken in remembrance of the great man of words. Instead, friends and accomplished musicians filled the room with jazz and blues—a reflection of Hughes's poetry and a tribute to his role in the Harlem Renaissance.

▼ **While in high school, Hughes trained as a junior military officer.**

For 20 years, Hughes was also a columnist for the *Chicago Defender*. This was a successful black newspaper. In his column, Hughes wrote about many subjects. Sometimes, he wrote about the dreams and struggles of the black community. Other times, he wrote about politics and justice. Hughes often wrote about civil rights and equality. Hughes was not afraid to say what was wrong with the way things were.

Hughes traveled and lived all over the world, including long periods of time spent in Harlem. Everywhere he went, he studied people closely. Hughes wrote about what he saw in different cultures and races. His writings informed and influenced people around the world. They are filled with deep, realistic observations on life. Hughes's writings are still as celebrated today as they were during the renaissance.

Zora Neale Hurston

Zora Neale Hurston was born in Alabama. When Hurston was old enough, she left home to travel the world. Hurston liked to meet and study people. She collected stories from many cultures. She was most interested in stories about African American people. Maybe it was these stories that inspired her to become a writer.

During Hurston's time, it was rare for women to go to college. It was even rarer for black women to go to college. But Hurston earned a degree from Howard University in 1920. Soon after, she moved to Harlem. It was there that she really began her career as a writer.

Hurston's home became a place for friends and writers to meet. They shared ideas and supported each other. Hurston's work began to be published in popular magazines. People could read her writings in *Opportunity* and *The Journal of American Folklore*. She and her friends, such as Langston Hughes, lived exciting lives. They were at the center of Harlem in its rebirth.

◀ **Hurston in 1940**

Gwendolyn Bennett

Gwendolyn Bennett was born in Texas. She was a celebrated journalist, poet, and painter of the renaissance. Bennett was college educated and also studied in Paris, France. Along with her many other achievements, she was also the head of the Harlem Community Art Center.

Countee Cullen

Countee Cullen was another celebrated poet and playwright of the Harlem Renaissance. He married Nina Yolande Du Bois—the daughter of W. E. B. Du Bois. Many people considered this the union of old and new black culture. The wedding was a huge society event.

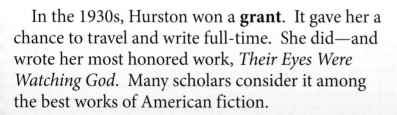

In the 1930s, Hurston won a **grant**. It gave her a chance to travel and write full-time. She did—and wrote her most honored work, *Their Eyes Were Watching God*. Many scholars consider it among the best works of American fiction.

Madam Walker

Madam C. J. Walker was a self-made millionaire at a time when that was nearly impossible for a black woman. She used part of her wealth to support the advancement of African American people. When she died, her daughter turned Walker's New York City mansion into a meeting place for members of the renaissance.

Harlem Globetrotters

A famous basketball team was founded in 1926—but not in Harlem. The Harlem Globetrotters team began in Chicago. But the team took the name "Harlem" to honor the cultural revolution that was happening at the time.

The Renaissance Lives On

The explosion of culture that was the Harlem Renaissance made waves throughout the world. Although the rebirth of art slowed during the Great Depression, it never died. From then until now, the creative output of black artists has flourished. It is the artists and scholars of the Harlem Renaissance who helped to make this possible.

Take a look at African American history. It's a history that includes the enslavement of an entire race of people. It's a history of countless numbers of people who were kept from fulfilling their dreams. The impact of the Harlem Renaissance cannot be overstated. There is no changing history and no way to rediscover what was lost. But perhaps the voices of the Harlem Renaissance have allowed us to imagine and shape a better future. Perhaps the dream once deferred is now a dream being realized.

Listen! Can you hear it?

Hurry! Get on now, it's coming.

Listen to those rails a-thrumming.

Oh boy, get on the A train.

Soon you will be on Sugar Hill in Harlem.

Sing It!

Great jazz and blues singers of the Harlem Renaissance sometimes sang in scat. To *scat* is to sing random syllables that don't have meaning but—when sung in a jazz or blues style—echo the wail, thump, and thrum of instruments. Scatting done well inspires a feeling and may even tell a story!

Listen to scatting in some classic songs. When you hear singers break into scat, you may want to scat along yourself. Give it a try! Pick a jazz or blues song from the Harlem Renaissance, such as one of these classics:

* ✱ "What a Little Moonlight Can Do"—Billie Holiday

* ✱ "Ain't Misbehavin'"—Louis Armstrong

* ✱ "How High the Moon"—Ella Fitzgerald

Select a section from your song and write a scat for it. Once it is written, practice your scat. Then perform it! After you've performed, push yourself even further to perform improvisational scats. Play an old jazz instrumental piece, such as one of these:

* ✱ "The Harlem Strut"—James P. Johnson

* ✱ "Ham and Eggs"—Jelly Roll Morton

* ✱ "East St. Louis Toodle-Oo"—Duke Ellington

Scat to the sound, and as you do, try to tell a story. You might even challenge your friends to a "scat off" and see who can come closest to Fitzgerald, Armstrong, and other greats in their scatting abilities!

Ella Fitzgerald

Glossary

blackface—dark makeup worn to give the look of very dark skin

bouncers—workers hired to keep people out of businesses, usually clubs or bars

cultural awakening—a discovery, a revival, or an embracing of something from a culture, including literature, art, music, language, and more

dean—someone who is in charge of part or all of a university, college, or school

deferred—postponed

genres—categories or types, especially of literature, music, and other art forms

grant—money or scholarship offered for a particular purpose

improvisational—describes a performance that is done without preparation

literary—having to do with written materials, usually in the form of stories, poems, and plays

mainstream—having to do with the largest number of people in a society

oppression—unfair, cruel treatment of a person or group

orchestra—a group of musicians who play together and who are led by a conductor

playwright—a person who writes plays

polyphonic—having many sounds and melodies played or sung simultaneously

scat—a jazz style of singing, which uses nonsense syllables but allows emotion to help tell a story

segregation—the practice of keeping people of different races, religions, or other groups separate from one another

social order—the system of human relationships within a society

swing—an upbeat rhythm that is played mostly for dancing

syncopated—music in which the weak beats are stressed instead of the strong beats

Index

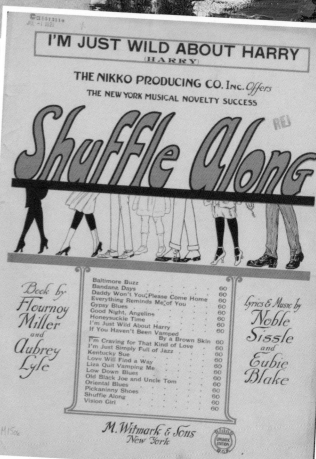

Your Turn!

When *Shuffle Along* first showed on Broadway, it marked a new day for the country. It was the first show written by, produced by, and starring black people. In what ways could something like that make a difference?

Imagine you are a newspaper reporter in 1921. Write an editorial (opinion piece) about why *Shuffle Along* is important not only for Broadway but also for the country as a whole.